Guide to Frank Lloyd Wright's California

GUIDE TO FRANK LLOYD WRIGHT'S

WRIGHT'S

CALIFORNIA

Text and photographs by Scot Zimmerman

Introduction by Arthur Dyson

GIBBS·SMITH PUBLISHER

First edition
95 94 93 92   5 4 3 2 1

This is a Peregrine Smith Book, published by
Gibbs Smith, Publisher
P.O. Box 667
Layton, UT 84041

Design by Kristin Bernhisel-Osborn

Cover photographs by Scot Zimmerman

Manufactured in the United States of America

**Library of Congress Cataloging-in-Publication
Data**

Zimmerman, Scot.
      Guide to Frank Lloyd Wright's
      California / Scot Zimmerman.
             p. cm.
      Includes index.
      ISBN 0-87905-448-4 (pbk.) : $14.95
      1. Architect-designed houses—
      California—Guidebooks.
2. Architecture, Modern—20th century—
California. 3. Wright, Frank Lloyd, 1867-
1959. I. Title.
NA7235.C2Z5 1992
728'.37'092—dc20   91-37414
                      CIP

Contents

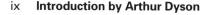

ix   **Introduction by Arthur Dyson**

2   **Southern California**
■■■

     4   **George C. Stewart Residence**
        196 Hot Springs Road, Montecito

     8   **Arch Oboler Gatehouse and Studio**
        32436 West Mulholland Highway, Malibu

     12   **George D. Sturges Residence**
        449 Skyewiay Road, Brentwood

     16   **Aline Barnsdall Residence (Hollyhock House)**
        4808 Hollywood Boulevard, Los Angeles

     20   **Charles Ennis Residence**
        2607 Glendower Avenue, Los Angeles

     24   **Samuel Freeman Residence**
        1962 Glencoe Way, Hollywood

     28   **John Storer Residence**
        8161 Hollywood Boulevard, Hollywood

     32   **Anderton Court Shops**
        332 Rodeo Drive, Beverly Hills

     36   **Alice Millard Residence (La Miniatura)**
        645 Prospect Crescent, Pasadena

     40   **Wilbur C. Pearce Residence**
        5 Bradbury Hills Road, Bradbury

     44   **Kundert Medical Clinic**
        1106 Pacific Street, San Luis Obispo

48   **Northern California / Bay Area**
■■

     50   **Clinton Walker Residence**
        Scenic Road at Martin Way, Carmel

     54   **Arthur C. Mathews Residence**
        83 Wisteria Way, Atherton

58   **Paul S. and Jean R. Hanna Residence (Honeycomb House)**
     737 Frenchman's Road, Stanford

62   **Sidney Bazett Residence**
     101 Reservoir Road, Hillsborough

66   **V. C. Morris Gift Shop**
     140 Maiden Lane, San Francisco

70   **Robert Berger Residence**
     259 Redwood Road, San Anselmo

74   **Marin County Civic Center**
     San Pedro Road at U.S. Highway 101, San Rafael

78   **Hilary and Joe Feldman Residence**
     13 Mosswood Road, Berkeley

82   **Maynard P. Buehler Residence**
     6 Great Oak Circle, Orinda

86   **Central California / San Joaquin Valley / Sacramento Valley**
■

88   **Pilgrim Congregational Church**
     2850 Foothill Boulevard, Redding

92   **Robert G. Walton Residence**
     417 Hogue Road, Modesto

96   **Randall Fawcett Residence**
     21200 Center Avenue, Los Banos

100 **George Ablin Residence**
     4260 Country Club Drive, Bakersfield

105 **Index**

Insight is the magical moment that brings consciousness to life. All else can serve only as a guide to lead us to the possibility of this inner transformation that makes the world seem something vitally fresh and new. What changes, of course, is not the world but our perception of ourselves.

One of the oldest wisdoms is that to know something you must experience it yourself. The depth and effectiveness of the insight often depends on the proficiency of the guide that brings us to the point of revelation. In architecture, that point must always be at the site of the building. The recognition of the need for direct experience, along with the practical difficulties of locating specific buildings, has been the inspiration for this guide to the architecture of Frank Lloyd Wright in California by the acclaimed architectural photographer, Scot Zimmerman.

Once while I was working with Mr. Wright, he commented that photographs often fail to convey the environment, the movements of people and sounds, the animals, plants, and climatic conditions that were always so integral to his architectural conceptions. He said, "If one would get the essential character of an organic building, it could not be by camera, inasmuch as it is wholly a matter of experience." Buildings, like all things, possess many unique qualities known only by their presence and not by abstraction into a secondary medium. Artistic expression is nevertheless the best hope for gaining the impression that can most accurately get us from here to there, where the magic awaits.

Architectural photography is one of the most difficult and

challenging of artistic efforts. Scot Zimmerman's skill can be seen in his first book, the highly prized *Romanza: The California Architecture of Frank Lloyd Wright,* as well as in the world's leading architectural journals. His ability to frame the spirit of structures is renown in architectural circles around the globe. His art is the art of enticement—the ability to spark a compelling relationship between the seeker and the space that creates an urge to remove the hurdle of distance.

Mr. Zimmerman's recognition of the importance of these architectural experiences, combined with his willingness to share, enables this book to bring many to the verge of architectural insight. He does not pretend to do more than that, but his guidance to these buildings is among the best possible.

Even the skills of a master photographer, however, cannot fully match the experience of visiting the buildings themselves. As in our acquisition of insight, the true value of the experience is the space within. As Mr. Wright wrote, "One must be in the building before one can understand what makes it what it is. Only when the buildings are comprehended from within and each in its place a feature of its own special environment—serving its own appropriate purpose with integrity—are they really seen."

By the use of light and shadow, materials and space, Frank Lloyd Wright established relationships that work psychologically and physiologically on us to stimulate our spirit through our senses. His work is a masterful, magnificent interplay of rhythms that respond to our deeper needs as human beings. By establishing an expression of intuitive emotions, Mr. Wright creates a poetic environment to be known only through itself. Because Scot Zimmerman knows this, too, he has presented this poem of his own.

You will be pleased to find that many of these wonderful buildings will be accessible to you. Within their walls you will experience the dramatic orchestration of light, planes, and materials that transform the merely physical into a true work of architecture. As noted by Mr. Zimmerman, many of these treasures retain their intended use, serving as private residences. The owners have graciously allowed their homes to be photographed and shared. In return and in appreciation for their generosity, I reiterate Scot Zimmerman's request to respect their privacy.

Visit the sites, appreciate the harmony of the design, open your senses. The Master will tantalize your perceptions with the gift of insight. The guide who has done his own work so well should also be appreciated.

Arthur Dyson, Architect
Fresno, California

Guide to Frank Lloyd Wright's California

California

Central California

Northern California

Southern California

Southern California

1. George C. Stewart, Montecito
2. Arch Oboler, Malibu
3. George D. Sturges, Brentwood
4. Aline Barnsdall (Hollyhock House), Hollywood
5. Charles Ennis, Los Angeles
6. Samuel Freeman, Hollywood
7. John Storer, Hollywood
8. Anderton Court Shops, Beverly Hills
9. Alice Millard (La Miniatura), Pasadena
10. Wilbur C. Pearce, Bradbury
11. Kundert Medical Clinic, San Luis Obispo

Guide to Frank Lloyd Wright's Southern California

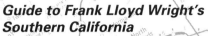

The strong horizontal lines of the redwood
board and batten exterior reflect the simplicity
of design Wright had often employed in his
lakeshore summer houses of the upper
Midwest. Though Wright continued to use
Prairie elements in his California work, the
strong midwestern features evident in the
Stewart house gave way, in later projects, to
his desire for a new form of regional
architecture.

George C. Stewart, 1909
196 Hot Springs Road
Montecito

Directions:

The Stewart house is fairly easy to locate. From the 101 freeway south of Santa Barbara exit at Coast Village Road. Go east on Hot Springs Road. The house is on a corner lot just a few blocks up from Coast Village Road.

The home faces east, so it is best to arrive in the morning for photographs. Parking is easy on Hot Springs Road. As the weather is beautiful year round in the Santa Barbara area, almost any time is a good time to see the Stewart house.

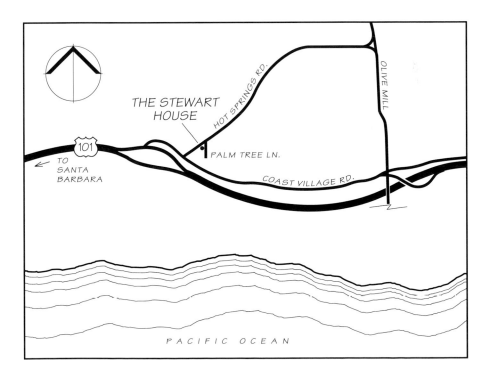

Description:

6 The original client, George Stewart, commissioned Wright to build the home as a winter retreat from the Midwest where his family lived in another of Wright's designs. Wright's first finished commission on the West Coast, it is similar in concept to his Prairie homes of the same era. It is also the first all-redwood home he designed for California.

Though designs for the Stewart house were finished shortly before Wright went to Europe to prepare the drawings for his Wasmuth portfolio of 1910, no one from Wright's office supervised construction, and many modifications were made. Over the years there have been other additions to and changes from the original plans to accommodate the different families who have called it home, but the house still retains its unmistakable style and beauty. It was recently purchased by Jerry Peterson who, with his daughter Nancy, has lovingly restored much of it to its original state. It is a private home and is opened on a very limited basis.

The two-story living room, its marvelous space flanked by the dining and reception rooms, lies at the heart of a cross-shaped floorplan. On the second story are two sleeping porches (which were enclosed in glass, deviating from Wright's design). Behind the living room is a much-modified service wing, in which Wright's garage has become a modern kitchen.

**196 Hot Springs Road
Montecito**

Redwood steps ascend to a back balcony shaded now by lush vegetation. A non-native pine forest has grown up enough in the eighty years since construction to block the view from the house toward the ocean.

A rock chimney seems to grow organically out
of the ground on this site—supporting the
hovering wings of the roofline. Wright
explored this use of masonry to connect a
building to its ground in several projects
accomplished during this period.

Arch Oboler, 1940-1941
32436 West Mulholland Highway
Malibu

Directions:

From the Ventura Freeway (101), exit on Westlake Village Boulevard and go south toward the ocean. Bear west (right) at the intersection of Westlake Village and Mulholland. The house is on the ocean side of the road several miles from this intersection.

You can park on Mulholland, but watch out for speeding cars. You can see the gatehouse (1940) from the road, and below it is a small wood and stone "retreat" or studio, built in 1941 and added to in 1944 and 1946. The view of Malibu and the Pacific Ocean is unobstructed. The property was recently sold and is currently under restoration. Access is limited so the buildings are difficult to photograph.

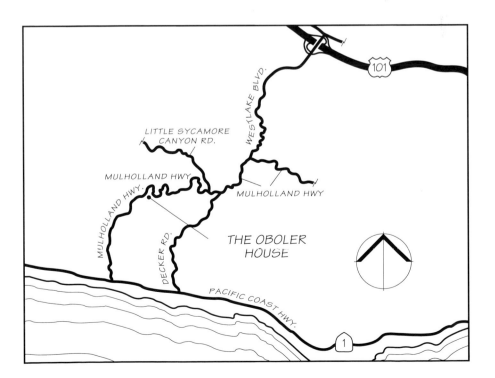

The small studio hangs like a
pavilion on the edge of the dry
hillside.

32436 West Mulholland Highway
Malibu

Description:

Arch Oboler, who was for years the voice of the radio show "Inner Sanctum and Lights Out," commissioned Wright to design his estate in 1940 in this setting of chaparral punctuated with rocky outcroppings. Dramatic tension is contained in the contrasting cantilevered wooden roof and the rubblestone walls.

Although Wright's spectacular projections for the main house, "Eagle Feather," were never realized, other segments of the complex were completed. Los Angeles architectural great John Lautner supervised construction.

A cool green pool at the eastern edge of the gatehouse reflects the sky and vegetation surrounding the theatrical structures.

The architect's sense of play is apparent: at the
entrance the brick house seems substantial and
grounded, yet on the public side it is all
hovering balcony, balustrade, and glass doors.

George D. Sturges, 1939
449 Skyewiay Road
Brentwood

Directions:

From the San Diego Freeway (405), exit at Sunset Boulevard and head west. Turn north on Kenter Avenue to Bonhill Road. Once you turn east (right again) on Skyewiay Road, you will have no trouble finding this house.

Parking is easy on the street. The house photographs well all year. It is a private home currently owned by two Hollywood greats and is not open for tours. Please don't intrude.

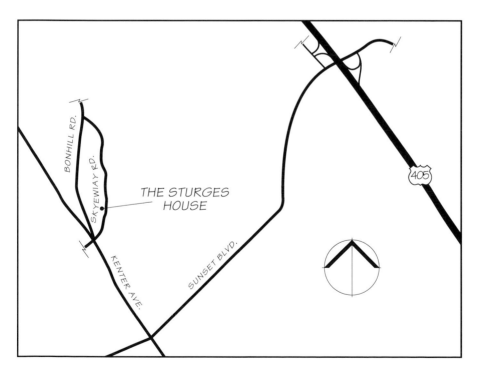

Description:

14 Dramatically cantilevered on the side of a hill, the Sturges house represents a departure from Wright's earlier Los Angeles area designs. Though neither as poetically placed nor as expensive as Fallingwater, the Sturges house is comparable to it in many ways.

Commissioned by a young engineer and his wife who saw Wright's work in a magazine, Wright summoned his sense of whimsy and fun to create a symbolic abstraction of the machine age through the eyes of a craftsman. The small scale of the interior is accentuated by the architect's furniture and the dark horizontal redwood walls held together with cadmium-plated screws. The living room calls to mind the inside of a finely-crafted yacht—built for speed. The exterior resembles a futuristic flying machine.

From the street, the Sturges
house appears windowless,
though all the major rooms
open on to a wraparound deck.

**449 Skyewiay Road
Brentwood**

The simple confidence of
wooden beam, post, and open
porch roof contrasts sharply
with the precarious balance of
house on the hillside.

Wright himself dubbed the building "Hollyhock House." His stylized version of that flower is the unifying ornamental motif. R.M. Schindler supervised construction of the main house while Wright was in Japan. He also built two satellite residences (A and B), and with the help of Richard Neutra, designed the wading pool and pergola.

Aline Barnsdall (Hollyhock House), 1917-1921
4808 Hollywood Boulevard
Los Angeles

Directions:

Hollyhock House and its Guest Residence are located in Barnsdall Art Park in the eastern part of Hollywood. From the Golden State Freeway (I-5), take the Los Feliz Boulevard exit west, just south of Griffith Park. Go west on Los Feliz to Vermont Avenue, south on Vermont to Hollywood Boulevard, then west half a block until you come to the entrance of Barnsdall Art Park on the south. There is a parking lot at the house, but do lock your car.

Aline Barnsdall deeded her estate to the city of Los Angeles in 1927; since then it has been a public park. The home is open for tours Tuesday through Sunday at 12, 1, 2, and 3 P.M. Call (213) 485-4581 for more information. The concrete and plaster exterior does not photograph well during the rainy season.

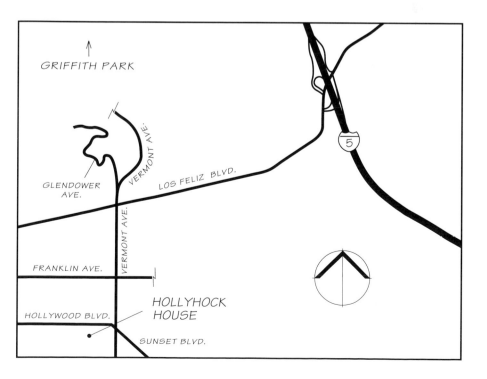

Built in a classic T-shaped plan, the Barnsdall house opens to shallow reflecting pools on both ends of the long axis. The central garden court gives onto a round pool on the east, and glass doors on the west end of the living room reveal a square pool. On the south is a walled patio.

▨ Description:

Hollyhock House, possibly the most famous of Wright's West Coast designs, was built for oil heiress Aline Barnsdall in between 1919 and 1921. Barnsdall originally intended to create an artist's community atop Olive Hill. Two additional residences, a pergola, and a children's wading pool were built, but the concept was never realized.

Though Wright's drawings of the Barnsdall house illustrated his chapter on the uses of concrete contained in "In the Cause of Architecture," the home is actually constructed with a variety of materials— from reinforced concrete to hollow tile and stucco-covered wood. The main house (which had crumbled badly) was restored in the seventies by Wright's son, Lloyd. Some of the furniture is original, including dining room chairs with hollyhock backs, and other pieces have been reconstructed. The high drama of Wright's conception is revealed in the house's great living spaces—and in such touches as the moat in front of the fireplace.

4808 Hollywood Boulevard
Los Angeles

Lying northeast of the main house, Residence A, now called the Barnsdall Arts Center, was originally built as a separate guest house. It was one of two designed and built on the property by Schindler under Wright's supervision (the other was torn down in the fifties).

The pyramid-stepped walls suggest the
platforms of archaeological sites in the jungles
of Central America. The romance of this
modern Mayan temple looking down from its
own mountain is intensified by its proximity to
the Hollywood hills.

Charles Ennis, 1924–1926
2607 Glendower Avenue
Los Angeles

Directions:

From Hollyhock House, head north on Vermont. Go through the intersection at Los Feliz toward the Greek Theatre in Griffith Park. Turn left off Vermont on Glendower Avenue. Follow Glendower as it meanders up the hill. You can see the house on top of the ridge— on the west side of the street.

The residence is currently being restored. Its owner, Gus Brown, gave it to a private trust in 1980. Call (213) 660-0607 for information about tours. Currently they are offered on the second Saturday of odd-numbered months. Like the Barnsdall house, the Ennis/Brown house photographs better during the dry time of year. Parking is tough, find a spot where you won't get ticketed.

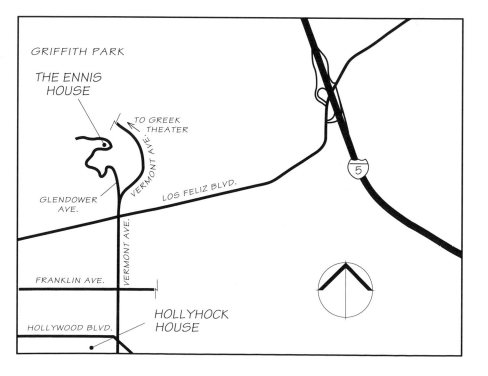

Description:

Situated in a commanding position on a ridge overlooking Hollywood, the massive size and pre-Columbian shape of the Ennis house caused a sensation when it was built—as it still does today. Though Wright had previously revealed his attachment to America's ancient architectural past in such early commissions as Midway Gardens in Chicago (1914), and later in the Hollyhock and Millard houses in California, this house is certainly the most theatrical of his "knitblock" constructions.

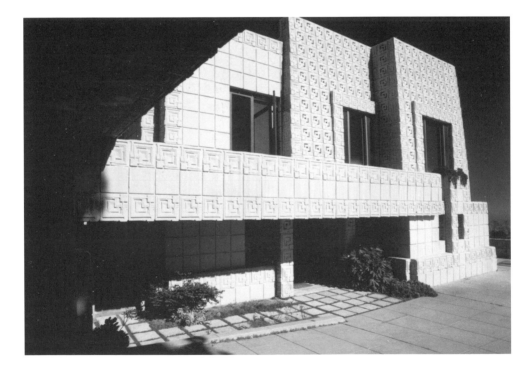

Alternating bands of plain and patterned concrete blocks encourage a dramatic interplay of light. Over the years, wind and weather have caused some deterioration; many of the blocks have been painted over with a preserving sealer.

In his autobiography Wright referred to the Ennis house as "the little palace." Once on the hill, the layers of retaining walls and parapets give way to horizontal spaciousness.

2607 Glendower Avenue
Los Angeles

Intimate interiors—warm, airy, and inviting—
characterize the Freeman house. "Concrete is
a plastic material," Wright wrote, "susceptible
to the impressions of the imagination."

Samuel Freeman, 1924–1925
1962 Glencoe Way
Hollywood

▌Directions:

After exiting the Hollywood Freeway (101) south on Highland
Avenue, proceed south to Franklin Avenue. Turn right on Franklin
and immediately right again on Hillcrest Road. The next right is
Glencoe Way, and the house it at the bottom of the curve.

Harriet P. Freeman gave her house to the School of Architecture at
the University of Southern California in 1984. You can call (213)
851-0671 for recorded information about scheduled tours. It is best
photographed in dry weather. Parking nearby is almost impossible.
Leave your car around the corner and walk up to it.

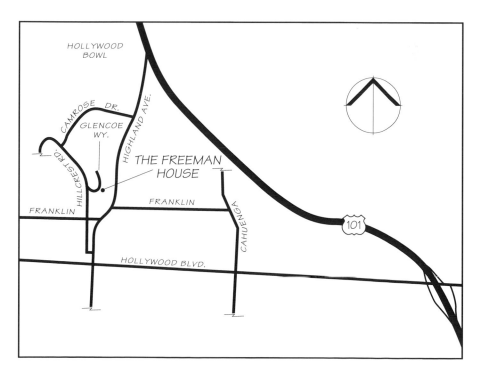

Some of Wright's eclectic
architectural influences
merge: pre-Columbian blocks
meet Asian-influenced
perforated screens.

Description:

At 1200 square feet, the Freeman house is the smallest
of the concrete-block houses Wright designed in Los
Angeles—and one of the most adventurous. Built on a
steep lot, it affords privacy from the street while
inviting the mild Southern California climate inside.
Generous expanses of glass soften the massive block
construction, imparting a human scale both inside and
out. Much of the furniture—both built-in and
freestanding—was designed by R.M. Schindler.
Wright's son, Lloyd, supervised construction; his
attention to landscape details helps the house—with all
its terraces—blend into the hillside.

Encouraged by glass set
within perforated blocks or
framed by metal mullions, the
visitor perceives concrete
walls as light screens rather
than heavy shields. Strong
horizontal lines and glass
corners open the inside and
invite the occupants to
participate in the outdoors.

A two-story living space, which opens onto terraces front and rear, dominates the interior. The low bedroom wing to the west and service wing to the east reinforce this central verticality.

John Storer, 1923–1924
8161 Hollywood Boulevard
Hollywood

Directions:

From the Hollywood Freeway (101), exit west on Hollywood
Boulevard. Go through downtown Hollywood to the intersection of
Laurel Canyon. Turn north to the first place you can legally make a
U-turn, then south back toward Los Angeles. Make a very quick
right (west) up the hill back onto Hollywood Boulevard. Wind
around a couple of blocks; the house is on the north.

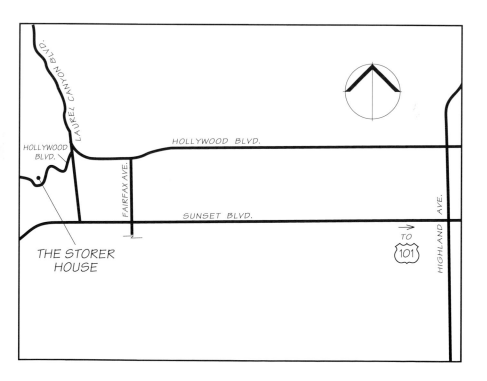

Description:

30   The Storer house, second of Wright's textured block houses in Los Angeles, is a fine example of "organic architecture"—situated as it is on the lot to take advantage of a beautiful view of Hollywood. Perforated blocks with the cedar windows and doors form a rich palate of materials. Original construction was supervised by Lloyd Wright, who also carried out some restoration in the early seventies. The house has been restored to its original grandeur by the current owner, Joel Silver, with help from Wright's grandson, Eric Lloyd Wright.

The "knitblock" system of construction (which Wright developed) consisted of two parallel rows of four-inch concrete block separated by a cavity filled with air. The two walls were "knitted" and reinforced with steel rods. Some blocks were smooth and some were patterned; others had the patterns perforated through the block and sealed internally with glass.

The stepped entrance and garden plots were planned by Lloyd Wright.

Though the terraced walls and pre-Columbian pattern are similar to the Ennis house of the same year, this house also shares much in common with the California Period houses which are its contemporaries.

8161 Hollywood Boulevard
Hollywood

At night, the illuminated Anderton Court reveals an intriguing array of windows on interior space.

Anderton Court Shops, 1952
332 Rodeo Drive
Beverly Hills

Directions:

From the San Diego Freeway (405), exit east at Santa Monica Boulevard. Follow Santa Monica Boulevard into Beverly Hills. Go south on Rodeo Drive three blocks. Anderton Court Shops are on the east and easy to find.

Park your car around back and take the time to stroll through Anderton's multi-level courts. The building is open year round. It faces west and photographs well in early evening.

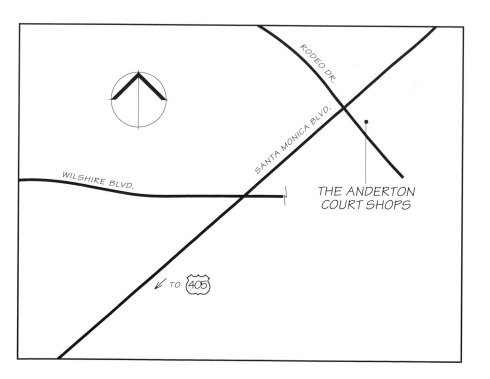

The narrow, yet open ramp
system and a small sunken
garden suggest a
neighborhood within the city.

332 Rodeo Drive
Beverly Hills

Description:

The only shopping plaza Wright designed for
California, Anderton Court has received little
attention. The mastlike tower and patterned fascia,
which were originally turquoise-colored fiberglass, are
painted white at this time. The design remains fresh in
conception, a vertical urban center, with four levels of
shops and offices connected by a winding ramp.

The futuristic tower serves
dramatically to advertise the
building, and although an
added canopy and signs have
compromised Wright's
design, it remains a delightful
building in a dynamic city.

A poetic setting surrounded by lush vegetation
lends an aura of mystery to "La Miniatura."

Alice Millard (La Miniatura), 1923
645 Prospect Crescent
Pasadena

Directions:

From the Ventura Freeway (134) exit east at Colorado Boulevard. Turn north (left) on North Orange Grove Boulevard, go past the Gamble House on the left, then turn left again on Prospect Boulevard to Prospect Crescent. Parking on the street is allowed, but this is a private home. Please don't disturb the occupants. Best photos are obtained in spring and summer.

The home can also be seen from Rosemont Avenue through the gate. This famous view shows a balcony overlooking the pond, and a studio built by Lloyd Wright.

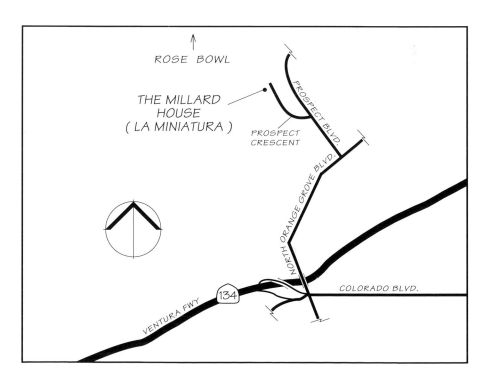

Description:

38 Wright's first realized "textile-block" house on the West Coast is one of the architectural gems of Southern California. Situated in a small, heavily-wooded ravine on a quiet circle and overlooking a pond, it is also the most romantic of his twenties block houses.

Built in 1923 for Alice Millard (who also owned a Frank Lloyd Wright home in Illinois), the home is being restored by its current owner. Consistent with his organic approach, Wright mixed sand from the site into the concrete for this and all of his Los Angeles block houses. He wanted to make sure the color and texture of the block would be compatible with the surrounding soil. Lloyd Wright supervised the original construction and designed the landscaping.

A small lane adjoins the house on the north side; entry is gained through a paved court and under a low bridge which allows access from the house to a terrace on the roof of the garage. The walls—both inside and out—are made of thin concrete blocks with an air space between; thus the interior space is connected closely to the exterior space. The two-story living room features patterned perforated concrete blocks above glass doors.

645 Prospect Crescent
Pasadena

The central sunken cross in this block pattern alludes to the pre-Columbian architecture of southern Mexico, but as with all of Wright's historical antecedents, it has been transformed into something modern—a light, open perforated shell.

A projecting flat roof with wide fascia shades
and brings to ground the curved walls of the
house and the entrance carport.

Wilbur C. Pearce, 1950
5 Bradbury Hills Road
Bradbury

Directions:

Go east on the Foothill Freeway (210) to Mountain Avenue (just west of Duarte). Travel north on Mountain to Royal Oaks. Go east (a right turn) on Royal Oaks to Bradbury Hills Road. Turn left through the gate and go up the hill to the east.

Although the entrance to the neighborhood is often locked, you can gain access. Mr. Lewellyn Pearce (son of the original owners) knows a great deal about the home and will allow guests a tour on occasion. Call him at (818) 359-7693. It's best to visit in spring, parking is no problem.

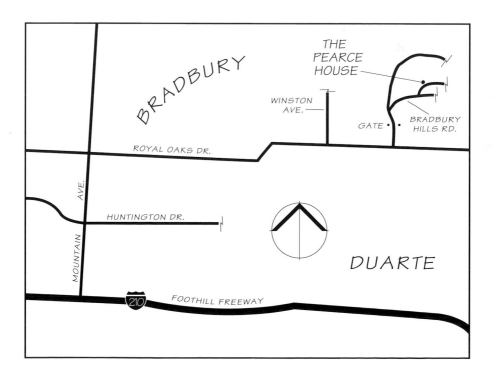

In the segmented circle scheme, a row of glass doors defines an inner circular wall, and behind these doors, serving as both living space and corridor, runs an open garden room. Behind the segmented curve lies the work space, while one end houses the covered entry and carport and the other is devoted to bedrooms.

5 Bradbury Hills Road
Bradbury

Description:

Located in the foothills of the San Gabriel Mountains, the house, with its large areas of glass on both sides, enjoys both a view toward Los Angeles (and on some days the ocean), and a view north into the mountains. All concrete-block construction, the Pearce house is one of a group of postwar designs in which Wright employed a Usonian scheme based on segments of a circle. In these houses, the classic L-shaped Usonian configuration is manipulated into a **C** shape, with an outdoor courtyard living space inside the curve.

A massive concrete-block fireplace is the focus of the living space at the center of the house.

The waiting room features an open clerestory with sawed-wood detailing, a warm wood ceiling, a brick fireplace, and furniture by Wright. A series of folding wood doors open on two sides to a patio partly screened by a wall and facing San Luis Creek.

Kundert Medical Clinic, 1954–1956
1106 Pacific Street
San Luis Obispo

Directions:

From 101, exit on Marsh Avenue. Go east to Santa Rosa Street, then turn south (right) and cross the bridge. The building is on the left at the corner of Santa Rosa and Pacific streets.

The owners are very proud and will let you tour the property, which is open daily during regular office hours. (But watch out for the dog across the creek when making photos!) You can park in the clinic's lot or on the street in front.

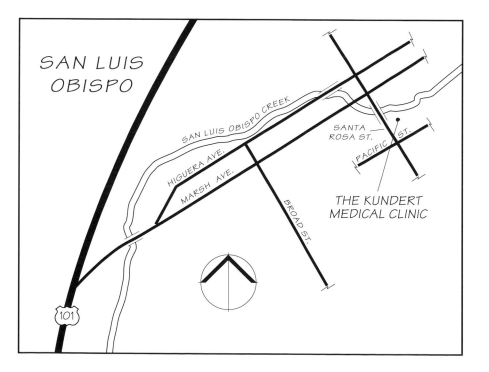

SAN LUIS
OBISPO

SAN LUIS OBISPO CREEK

HIGUERA AVE.

MARSH AVE.

BROAD ST.

SANTA
ROSA ST.

PACIFIC ST.

THE KUNDERT
MEDICAL CLINIC

101

Both inside and out, the
sawed-wood detailing and
raked-brick walls create
restful, inviting spaces.

1106 Pacific Street
San Luis Obispo

Description:

Though more domestic than commercial in scale, the public approach to Kundert Clinic betrays its function as the office of a dentist and an optometrist. Local building codes prevented Wright from executing his initial plans in patterned concrete block, so he translated the concept into wood and brick.

Though close to the center of town, the placement of the clinic in a grove of trees beside the stream suggests a rural setting.

Northern California/Bay Area

1. Clinton Walker, Carmel
2. Arthur C. Mathews, Atherton
3. Paul S. and Jean R. Hanna (Honeycomb House), Stanford
4. Sidney Bazett, Hillsborough
5. V. C. Morris Gift Shop, San Francisco
6. Robert Berger, San Anselmo
7. Marin County Civic Center, San Rafael
8. Hilary and Joe Feldman, Berkeley
9. Maynard P. Buehler, Orinda

Guide to Frank Lloyd Wright's
Northern California

The symphonic relationship of setting and
house are testimony to the success of Wright's
organic approach.

Clinton Walker, 1948
Scenic Road at Martin Way
Carmel

Directions:

From Highway 1 in Carmel, go west (curving northwest) to Rio Road. Turn west toward the ocean on Santa Lucia Avenue, then south at Scenic Road. The house is on the ocean side, one block from Santa Lucia. It is also accessible from the beach. Parking is available on the street in front. It photographs well all year, but be sure to respect the owner's privacy.

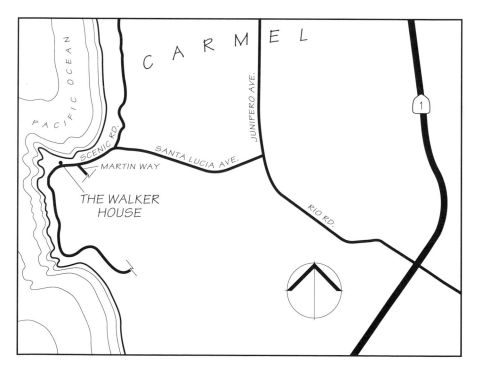

Description:

52 Growing from the rocks overlooking Monterey Bay, the house includes a living-dining room around a central fireplace, a utlilitarian kitchen behind, and beyond this core a gallery of three bedrooms. It has been enlarged slightly, but within the original 1200 square feet (carport included) Wright articulated a Usonian plan based on modular four-foot equilateral triangles. The detailed small spaces, and built-in furniture make the interior feel like a ship.

With its ship's prow terrace, and blue-green roof floating above a contrasting red soffit, the Walker home enjoys an unobstructed view of the ocean. Wright said of this house, "The overall effect is quiet, and the long white surf lines of the sea seem to join the lines of the house to make a natural melody."

Scenic Road at Martin Way
Carmel

Stepped out like inverted pyramids beneath the cantilevered overhang, windows set in thin, layered stone receive the ocean light.

The flatness of the terrain on which the house
is built is echoed thematically in the sweeping
expanses of lawn and terrace, and in the
strong horizontal statement of the low-pitched
roof.

Arthur C. Mathews, 1950
83 Wisteria Way
Atherton

Directions:

From the Bayshore Freeway (101), exit west at Willow Road (84). Take Willow Road west (southwest) to Middlefield Road. Turn right on Middlefield to Oak Grove Avenue, then right again on Oak Grove to Green Oaks Drive. Turn left on Green Oaks to Rosewood Drive, then right (the only way you can go) on Rosewood. Make a right turn on Wisteria Way and congratulations, you found it.

Because of the lush landscaping, the exterior of the Mathews home is difficult to photograph, and it is a private residence, not open to the public. You can park on the street in front, but watch out for the neighborhood children.

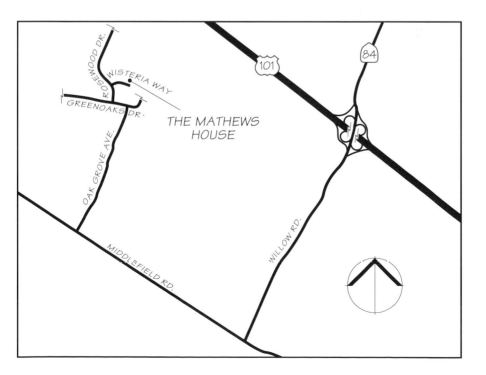

Wright's characteristically
massive chimney anchors the
house to the ground.

83 Wisteria Way
Atherton

Description:

The Mathews house is a beautiful low, raked-brick design based on the diamond created by two equilateral triangles. The living room and opposing bedroom wing extend out to define a private garden, which means the house can be completely open on the back, with floor-to-ceiling windows perfect for the mild Bay Area climate. The small windows visible from the street (which open for cross ventilation) and sawed-wood cutouts in the overhang provide interesting contrast to the soothing roof line.

A horizontal hedge planting complements the raked-brick walls.

Wright wrote that he used the hexagon in
preference to the common rectangle because it
was "consistent with a more human rhythm. . . .
All corners are obtuse as in the honeycombs,
therefore a pattern more natural to human
movement is the result."

Paul R. and Jean S. Hanna (Honeycomb House), 1936
737 Frenchman's Road
Stanford

█Directions:

From the Junipero Serra Freeway (280), exit east at Page Mill Road (G3). From the Bayshore Freeway (101) exit west at Oregon Expressway (which becomes Page Mill—G3). Follow Page Mill to Junipero Serra Boulevard. Exit north on Serra Boulevard and travel north (northwest) to Campus Drive. Make a sharp right turn on Campus Drive and follow it to Mayfield Avenue. Turn right on Mayfield to Frenchman's Road, then left on Frenchman's. The house is on the left about two blocks up.

Tours will resume when the damage sustained in the recent earthquake has been repaired. Call Stanford University for dates. (415) 723-2300.

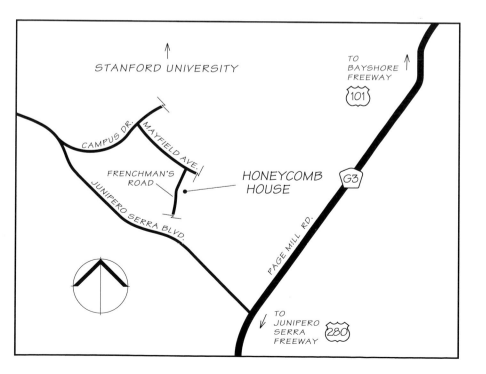

The vertical space of a central clerestory contrasts with the low ceilings which dominate the building. Though a brick exterior anchors the house in the hillside, many of the walls are made of thin layers of laminated wood so that they can be moved to rearrange the living space as children grow and needs change.

Description:

The Hanna house, now the residence of Stanford's provost, is one of Wright's most famous designs in California, and one of 17 structures designated by the American Institute of Architects as representative of Wright's contribution to American culture.

Built during the architect's Depression-era burst of creative energy, it was his first house in the Bay Area and one of the first hexagonal grid houses. It features an organization which became characteristic over the next 20 years—living spaces surrounding a central chimney mass behind (or in) which lies a skylit kitchen.

737 Frenchman's Road Stanford

The modular arrangement of repeated hexagons creates an open plan which projects the interior spaces out into terraces and views. A walled garden and a separate guest wing ground the house as it sits on the hill. On the other side, brick terraces make fabulous views and new living areas accessible.

The horizontal roof over the bedroom wing
creates a series of cubicles, while the exposed
gable roof in the living room defines public space.
As did many Usonian houses of the period, the
Bazett house contains a long built-in couch next to
the fireplace and above it a horizontal band of
windows covered by patterned wood screens.

Sidney Bazett, 1939
101 Reservoir Road
Hillsborough

Directions:

From Highway 92 (which crosses the San Mateo Bridge), exit north at Alameda de Las Pulgas. Continue on the Alameda until it ends at Crystal Springs Road. Go left at Crystal Springs to Ridgeway Road. Make the sharp right at Ridgeway and continue to Bowhill Road. Stay on Bowhill to Reservoir Road, then go left. The house is not visible from the street, but is on the left one quarter block up.

This is a private home, not open to the public. You can drive by and park on the street for a peek.

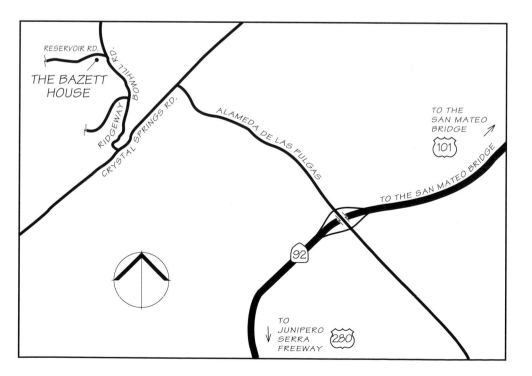

Description:

A smaller, conceptual cousin to the Hanna house, the Bazett home is also planned on the hexagonal module. Originally constructed for a client and his young bride, it was never occupied by them. The current owners have added a Wright-designed studio wing, and keep the home in pristine condition. It features beautiful built-in furniture, including a unique hexagonal steel bathtub. On the back it opens to lush plantings.

As in the Hanna house, raked brick constitutes the lower part of the walls, while the upper walls and roof are of laminated redwood. The glass windows and walls suggest an oriental garden house on a brick terrace.

101 Reservoir Road
Hillsborough

Wright recorded a number of design features he considered to be essential to his thirties Usonian house including this one: "Furniture, pictures, and bric-a-brac are unecessary because the walls can be made to include them or be them." But his concept of the affordable house was not trivial. In his mind the term was synonymous with democracy.

Inside is original furniture, a beautiful
suspended plastic ceiling, and an enclosed
spiral ramp (with peekholes) that winds up
through the art work on display.

V. C. Morris Gift Shop, 1948
140 Maiden Lane
San Francisco

▪Directions:

From the East Bay, take the Fifth Street exit off the Bay Bridge (I-80). Follow Fifth to Folsom Street. Go right on Folsom to Third Street. From the South Bay, take 101 to I-80 East, then the Fourth Street exit and Bryant Avenue to Third Street.

Go left on Third across Market Street to Geary Street. Turn left on Geary to Union Square where you can park your car in the garage and walk across Stockton Street to Maiden Lane. While interior photos are not allowed, you can take good exteriors from the street in early morning or late afternoon.

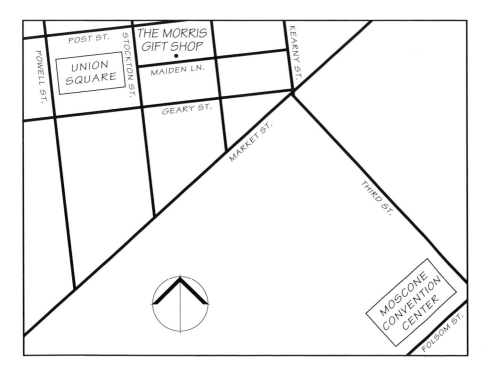

Faced with raked brick
dissected with illuminated
glass block, the exterior
features an arched entry
reminiscent of Louis Sullivan.

Description:

Originally a gift store selling fine glass and china, this remodeled warehouse is now the home of the Circle Gallery. A simple skylit cube, it is a must-see on your tour of the Bay Area—an artful lesson in the use of space. Call the gallery at (415) 989-2100.

140 Maiden Lane
San Francisco

Maiden Lane is a small one-way street on the east side of Union Square. The building is on the north side of Maiden Lane between Stockton and Grant streets.

In typical Usonian fashion, the plan calls for a
concealed workspace kitchen behind a
masonry fireplace, around which the living
spaces revolve.

Robert Berger, 1950
259 Redwood Road
San Anselmo

Directions:

From 101, exit west at Sir Frances Drake Boulevard. Go all the way through Ross to San Anselmo. Turn left at Red Hill Avenue, then left again on Madrone Avenue to Center Boulevard. Turn right on Center and follow it to Redwood Road where you'll make a left turn. Go slowly, it's a narrow winding climb up Redwood to the house.

This is a private home but the owner will usually let you visit. Parking is not as difficult as finding the house. It photographs well all year.

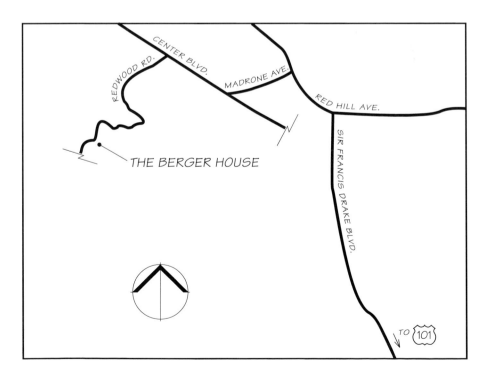

Description:

Robert Berger, a young and ambitious school teacher, commissioned Wright to design his dream home. He then built it himself—one wheelbarrow-load at a time. He and his young family camped in sleeping bags until the bedrooms could be completed. It may be the only residence in California with a Frank Lloyd Wright-designed doghouse.

The Bergers's Usonian doghouse.

Form-cast walls of concrete
and native stone make the
house look as though it is
emerging naturally from its
hilly, wooded site in Marin
County.

259 Redwood Road
San Anselmo

With their low archways, the two bridgelike
structures seem to spring from the hills like the
roads in a futuristic city.

Marin County Civic Center, 1957–1972
San Pedro Road at 101
San Rafael

75

Directions:

From 101, exit at San Pedro Road. Go east on San Pedro, then north (left) on Civic Center Drive.

This is a public complex, you can walk through it freely—though they will chase you out of the jail area. Be certain to see the rooftop garden and restaurant. You can also walk down to the lake and have lunch on the grass, taking in the impressive scale of this project. Parking is always easy, and any time is a good time to see it.

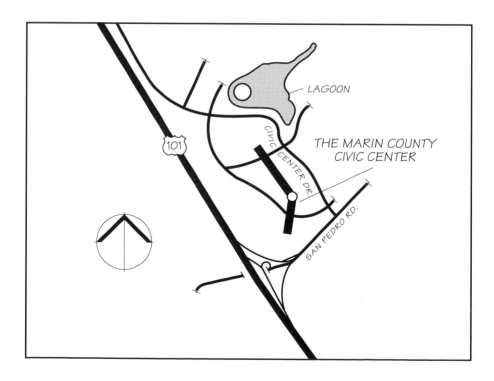

The civic center's tower,
visible for miles, is juxtaposed
to the rounded roof-lines and
soft archways, an echo of the
Moderne, machine-inspired
outlines of the 1930s which
symbolized the future.

San Pedro Road at 101
San Rafael

Description:

Under construction at the time of Wright's death in 1959, the Marin County Civic Center is one of his best-known California designs. The buildings were completed over fifteen years by associate architect, Aaron Green, along with Wright's son-in-law, Wes Peters. The whole complex expresses Wright's views about the importance of a middle-class citizen's activity in a true democracy, and calls to mind a scaled-down Broadacre, his idealized city.

The skylit atriums, admitting natural light, seem to banish bureaucracy.

Though Wright himself might have modified
this house had he supervised its construction,
the raked-bricked walls, patterned plywood
ceilings, and sawed-wood cutouts on the
kitchen screen (which are mirrored in the
clerestory and in some transoms) seem utterly
contemporary—not anachronistic, but
timeless.

Hilary and Joe Feldman, 1974
13 Mosswood Road
Berkeley

Directions:

From I-80 (580), exit east at University Avenue. Go east on University to Shattuck Avenue, then south (right) on Shattuck to Channing Way. Go left on Channing to Prospect Street, then left on Prospect to Orchard Lane. Turn right again up the hill to Mosswood Road, then left on Mosswood. The house is on the left at the turn.

Its current owners, top fashion designers who delight in owning the home, also delight in privacy, so please don't disturb them. Parking is tough as the dead-end street is narrow and winding. You can park on Prospect Street and walk up past the home on a public path just below.

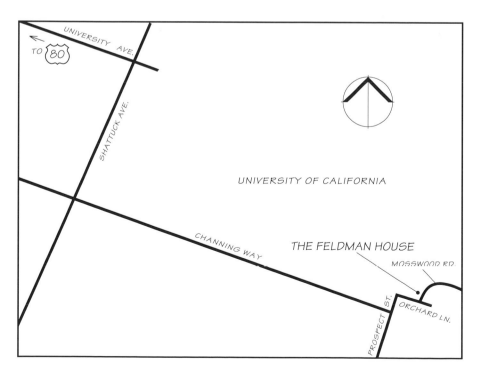

Description:

80   Built after Wright's death, the Feldman house, though created from a design planned for another site, fits its new environment well. The large central living area and clerestory open up to a spectacular view of the San Francisco Bay. It has a small private courtyard with built-in seating and a cantilevered carport roof.

One of the cantilevered roofs extends to shade the entrance and form the carport. A bank of windows in the living/dining room opens on to a brick terrace on the garden side.

13 Mosswood Road
Berkeley

From among Wright's unrealized plans, the Feldmans selected a 1939 design intended for a Los Angeles site, and built it in 1974 on this wooded hillside in Berkeley.

A terrace encloses the swimming pool,
accessible to the back side of the house and
adjacent to the long wing of bedrooms,
providing an ideal environment for outside
entertaining.

Maynard P. Buehler, 1948
6 Great Oak Circle
Orinda

Directions:

From Highway 24, exit at Moraga Way (the Orinda BART station exit). Go south on Moraga to Glorietta Boulevard. Turn left on Glorietta, then immediately left again on to Orchard Road. Great Oak Circle is on the left as soon as you turn on to Orchard.

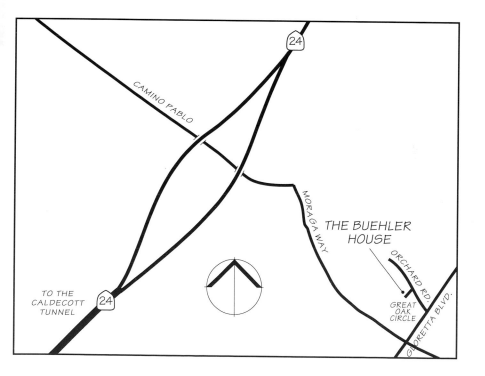

Lush growth on this site on
the hills of the East Bay
engulfs the Buehler house.

84

Description:

Built in 1948 for the Buehler family, this home is a
long, low, concrete-block and wood design on the
Usonian theme—with beautiful sawed-wood trim in
the entry and a perforated walkway cover. The home
features a wonderful Japanese garden and a complete
shop, for its owner is a world-renowned inventor.

A Usonian L-shaped plan is
crowned by the dramatic
living room set at an oblique
angle. Heavy concrete walls
are softened by the glass
and the thin, soaring
wooden roofline.

6 Great Oak Circle
Orinda

REDDING

**Central Valley/San Joaquin Valley/
Sacramento Valley**

MODESTO

LOS BANOS

BAKERSFIELD

1. Pilgrim Congregational Church, Redding
2. Robert G. Walton, Modesto
3. Randall Fawcett, Los Banos
4. George Ablin, Bakersfield

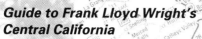

Guide to Frank Lloyd Wright's
Central California

A comfortable low entrance faces the parking area, inviting visitors to enter the triangularized tentlike space.

Pilgrim Congregational Church, 1958–1963
2850 Foothill Boulevard
Redding

Directions:

From I-5, exit at Eureka Way (299). Go west through town to
Almond Avenue. Go south on Almond one block to Foothill
Boulevard, then west on Foothill. The church is at the western end of
Foothill about one-half mile from the turn off of Eureka Way.

The building is open during office hours, call (916) 243-3121. Be
sure to see the original Wright drawings displayed inside. It
photographs well year round. Parking is easy in the adjacent church
lot. During the warm summer months Redding is consistently the
hottest city in the valley, so the best time to visit is early spring.

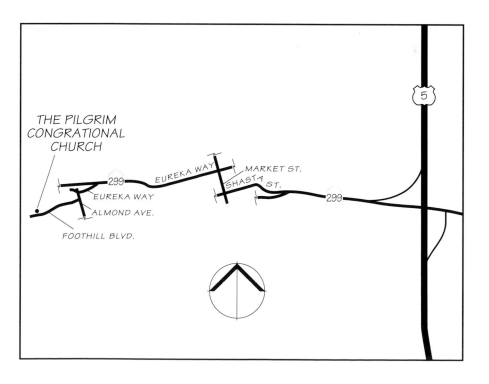

Description:

Though its design was finished just before Wright's death, the seldom-seen structure was never fully realized. Pilgrim consists of a chapel and attached offices of desert rubblestone. Its striking metal roof suspended from concrete poles mirrors the shape of nearby Mt. Shasta.

Wright's original design called for the construction of a central stone tower topped by a thin metal spire. The tower has never been built.

Wright designed four parts to this church—sanctuary, chapel, offices, and fellowship hall. The masonry walls of the completed structure marry it to the edge of a small river gorge.

2850 Foothill Boulevard
Redding

The house is composed of three parts,
including this striking living room area.

Robert G. Walton, 1957
417 Hogue Road
Modesto

Directions:

From 99, exit east at Kiernan Avenue (219). Go east on Kiernan to McHenry Avenue (108), then north on McHenry to Hogue Road. (Once you cross the river, you've gone too far.) Go east on Hogue, where you'll find the house on the north side, one block from McHenry.

The best time to visit is in the early spring. Photos of the Walton house are best made in early morning (pool area) or late afternoon (entry). It is a private residence and not generally open for tours. Parking is easy on the street.

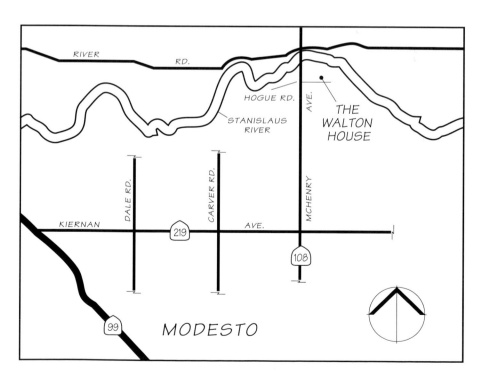

Description:

94　A long, low home designed for the San Joaquin Valley's climate and a large family, the Walton house is a beauty, one of the most rewarding of Wright's later projects. Rectangular in plan, with an L shape, it combines elements of Wright's early California houses of the twenties (patterned block, flat roofs, and parapets) in an enlarged version of the late-thirties classic Usonian scheme.

It also contains a great many pieces of Wright-designed furniture—both built-in and mobile—including wonderful wood chairs with high, slatted backs. The lovely site, with its slope toward the river covered with Valley Oak trees, is worth a visit on its own merits.

A courtyard leads to the
carport and exposes the
extended low-roofed
bedroom and playroom wing.

**417 Hogue Road
Modesto**

Full-length glass panels in the
back wall of the bedrooms
open on to the pool area and
the garden. A central
workspace core and parapet
houses—as it often does in
Wright's houses—the kitchen
and fireplace.

Steps surround the back of the home, leading
down from the dining room with its peaked roof
to the swimming pool, and from the living room
terrace to the garden.

Randall Fawcett, 1955
21200 Center Avenue
Los Banos

Directions:

From Pacheco Boulevard (152) in Los Banos, go south on Center Avenue 5.5 miles. The home is on the east, down a long driveway. It is a private residence, and not generally open for tours.

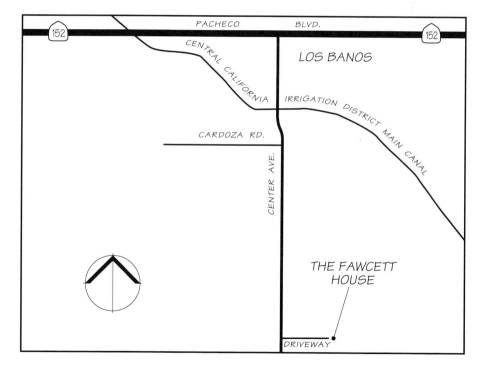

Perforations in the sheet-metal roof overhangs create light patterns on the shaded walkways. The home also boasts an abundance of sawed-wood detailing and a central living room with walk-in fireplace.

21200 Center Avenue
Los Banos

Description:

For a dairy-farming family Wright designed a long, low, concrete-block home that fits its site and uses perfectly. Dramatic angles and horizontal lines complement the landscape in this part of the San Joaquin Valley. The plan describes a shallow, expanded U shape arranged around a central garden and augmented by a carport and shop wing.

Entrance is gained through an angular, partially-covered loggia facing northwest.

The plan is a variation of Wright's triangular
module with a central pavilion housing the entry,
dining room, workspace, and the breathtaking
pitch-roofed living room. Two bedroom wings
flank the central living space.

George Ablin, 1958
4260 Country Club Drive
Bakersfield

Directions:

From 99, take 58 east toward Tehachapi. Exit 58 at Oswell Street. Go north on Oswell to Country Club Drive, then east on Country Club, past the Bakersfield Country Club on the left. The home, though difficult to see from the road, is also on the left, one mile from the Oswell intersection.

The owners, who are actively involved with the arts in Bakersfield, occasionally open the home for tours. It photographs well year round, but the best time to visit is in early spring.

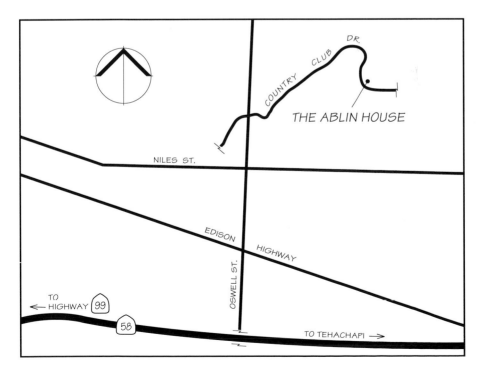

Description:

The Ablin house, one of Wright's last California
commissions, is a pomegranate-colored, cement-block
design for a dynamic, growing Bakersfield family. The
home appears low and attached to the ground with
deep roof overhangs which provide shade in a warm
climate. The central courtyard holds a triangular pool
and red concrete terraces.

The low, concrete walls with
perforated-block windows
shield occupants from a
suburban, country-club
setting while reinforcing the
intense beauty of the Central
Valley's strong light.

Patterns of light fall into the
kitchen workspace through
this perforated central
parapet.

4260 Country Club Drive
Bakersfield

Index

Ablin Residence, 100–103
American Institute of Architects, 60
Anderton Court Shops, 32–35
Arts and Crafts Center, 19
Asian, oriental (influence of), 65
Atherton, 55, 56

Bakersfield, 101, 102, 103
Barnsdall, Aline, 17, 18
Barnsdall Residence, 16–19, 21
Bay Area (San Francisco), 48, 56, 60, 69
Bay Bridge, 67
Bazett Residence, 62–65
Berger, Robert, 72
Berger Residence, 70–73
Berkeley, 79, 81
Beverly Hills, 33, 34
Bradbury, 41, 42
Brentwood, 13, 15
Broadacre, 77
Brown, Gus, 21
Buehler, Maynard P., 83, 84
Buehler Residence, 82–85

Caldecott Tunnel, 83
California Period, 31
Carmel, 51, 53
Central America (influence of), 20
Central California (section), 1, 86–103
Central Valley, 102
Chicago, 22

Duarte, 41
Dyson, Arthur (introduction by), ix–xi

Eagle Feather (Oboler), 11
East Bay (San Francisco), 67, 84
Ennis, Charles, 21, 23
Ennis Residence (Ennis/Brown), 20–23

Fallingwater, 14
Fawcett, Randall, 97
Fawcett Residence, 96–99
Feldman, Joe and Hilary, 79, 81
Feldman Residence, 78–81
Freeman, Harriet P., 25
Freeman Residence, 24–27

Gamble House, 37
Greek Theatre, 21
Green, Aaron, 77
Griffith Park, 17, 21

Hanna, Paul S. and Jean R., 59
Hanna Residence, 58–61, 64, 65
Hillsborough, 63, 65
Hollyhock House, 16–19, 22
Hollywood, 17, 19, 20, 25, 29
Honeycomb House, 58–61

Illinois, 38
"In the Cause of Architecture," 18

Japan (influence of), 16, 84

knitblock (system of construction), 22, 30
Kundert Medical Clinic, 44–47

La Miniatura, 36–39
Laurel Canyon, 29
Lautner, John, 11
Los Angeles, 14, 17, 21, 22, 23, 25, 27, 30, 38, 43, 81
Los Banos, 97, 98
Louis Sullivan, 68

Malibu, 9, 10
Marin County, 73, 74, 77
Marin County Civic Center, 74–77
Mathews, Arthur C., 55
Mathews Residence, 54–57
Mayan (influence of), 20
Mexico, 39
Midway Gardens, 22
Midwest, 4, 6
Millard, Alice, 37, 38
Millard Residence, 22, 36–39
Moderne (style), 76
Modesto, 93, 95
Montecito, 4, 7
Monterey Bay, 52
Morris, V.C. (Building), 69
Morris Gift Shop, 66–69
Mt. Shasta, 90

Neutra, Richard, 16
Northern California (section), 1, 48–85

Oboler, Arch, 9, 11
Oboler Gatehouse and Studio, 8–11
Olive Hill, 18
organic architecture, ix, 30, 37, 50
Orinda, 83, 85

Pacific Ocean, 5, 9, 43, 51
Pasadena, 41, 42
Pearce, Lewellyn, 41

106

Pearce, Wilbur, 41
Pearce Residence, 40–43
Peters, Wes, 77
Peterson, Jerry and Nancy, 6
Pilgrim Congregational Church, 88–91
Prairie style, 4, 6
pre-Columbian (influence of), 22, 26, 31, 39

Redding, 89, 91
regional architecture, 4
Romanza: the California Architecture of Frank Lloyd Wright, x
Ross, 71

Sacramento Valley, 86
San Anselmo, 71
San Francisco, 67, 69
San Francisco Bay, 80
San Gabriel Mountains, 43
San Joaquin Valley, 86, 94, 99
San Luis Creek, 44, 45
San Luis Obispo, 45, 46
San Mateo Bridge, 63
San Rafael, 75, 76
Santa Barbara, 5
Schindler, R. M., 16, 19, 26
Sidney Bazett, 63
Silver, Joel, 30
South Bay (San Francisco), 67
Southern California (section), 1, 2–47
Stanford, 59, 61
Stanford University, 59
Stanislaus River, 93
Stewart, George C., 5, 6
Stewart Residence, 4–7
Storer, John, 29
Storer Residence, 28–31
Sturges, George D., 13
Sturges Residence, 12–15

Union Square, 67, 69
University of California, 79
University of Southern California, 25
Usonian (concept of architecture), 43, 52, 62, 65, 70, 72, 84, 85, 94

Walker, Clinton, 51
Walker Residence, 50–53
Walton, Robert G., 93
Walton Residence, 92–95
Wasmuth portfolio, 6
West Coast, 6, 18, 38

Wright, Eric Lloyd, 30
Wright, Frank Lloyd, ix, x, 4, 11, 14, 16, 18, 22, 24, 34, 37, 39, 43, 44, 52, 53, 56, 58, 60, 64, 65, 72, 77, 78, 80, 81, 89, 90, 94, 95, 99, 100, 102; writings and quotations of, ix, x, 18, 24, 53, 58, 65
Wright, Lloyd, 19, 26, 30, 37

Zimmerman, Scot, ix, x, xi